Hong Kong Life Hacks: 15 Simple Things You NEED To Know Before Living in Hong Kong

By Dan K.W.P

You could scour the internet, searching hundreds of websites for the best tips and tricks before moving to Hong Kong, but that would take countless hours and a great deal of research. Instead of wasting your time doing that, hack your way to an easier life in Hong Kong using this valuable book.

The hard work has been done for you, gathering the best tips of living in Hong Kong from the author's own experience. You can relax, read, and plan your move to the city.

Author Dan K.W.P is a freelance journalist and multimedia content creator who's entering his fifth year of living in Hong Kong as an expat. He has published this book to help first-timers save money and save time in adjusting to Hong Kong.

With 15 genius, life-saving tips included, you are sure to find many things to implement and make your day-to-day living in Hong Kong better.

Grab this book today and start hacking your way to living your best life in the most exciting city of Asia!

ISBN: 9798649005661

Some of the opinions stated are based on the author’s observations alone and have not been independently verified.

This book is available in print or ebook format at amazon.com and other retailers.

I dedicate this book to Hong Kong,
Wishing the fastest recovery.

Table of Contents

1. Get a Dehumidifier.

Hong Kong is very humid.
It sometimes gets so humid that mere air conditioning just won't do the trick.
In 2019, the average humidity climbed over 80% from April to August.
Another reminder, Hong Kong has a very long summer.
So you will need to anticipate the long summer of heat and humidity.
With the heat and humidity combined with day to day living (hot showers, hanging wet clothes for them to dry, etc.), mold can easily form on the walls and ceilings.
So definitely, get a dehumidifier.
The price varies greatly from 600 HKD (Hong Kong dollars) to even 4000, but usually ones priced around 1000 HKD are the most effective.

2. Getting on and off the bus in Hong Kong.

This is the topic that has some sub-topics I want to go over with you guys.
In Hong Kong, there is the big, two-deck bus and the minibus.
Both types of buses accept the Octopus card or cash.
Keep in mind that most buses do not give you any change.
So make sure you have the right amount of money when paying with cash.
Regarding the cost, the cost of each bus ride differs and is very hard to predict.
The best thing you can do is to download the Citybus App on your phone to calculate how much it costs to get to your destination.
Now, there are buses that have the same number but with the alphabet X

behind it. X stands for express. It might skip the station you were aiming to get off, or it may have a completely different route to get to a certain station compared to the normal numbered. Also, they are more expensive.

In Hong Kong, there are some bus stations that if you don't wave at the bus, it won't stop.
Getting off a minibus is tricky. On the big bus, there is a bell and there is a screen showing the next few stations. There are neither on a minibus. So you always have to watch where the bus is heading closely. And to get off, you have to yell at the bus driver, "Next Stop Please" or " Yau Lok". If the driver doesn't hear you, he will just keep on driving.

3. VISAs cannot be extended if you're not physically in Hong Kong to collect them.

For students that study beyond the expected period of 4 years, they need to extend their student visas.

Often I hear my fellow expat friends areout of Hong Kong at the time for extension.

To extend the visa, you need to pick up the processed visa in person.

If you are away, what you can do is apply for a new visa. You can apply for a new visa before the expiration of your current visa, and have the new one mailed to you wherever you are.

4. Uber IS available in Hong Kong

Taxis are easy to find in Hong Kong, as there are so many. But if you don't speak Cantonese, you can sometimes encounter some difficult situations from miscommunication. And taxis in Hong Kong does not accept electronic payment, credit/debit cards or Octopus cards.

Just to let you know, Uber is available in Hong Kong. There is also a local app named HKTaxi, which has over 50,000 registered taxis.

Using these apps can help you with planning since it tells you how much the trip will cost before you get on. There's a fixed amount of cost for the trip.

Meanwhile, regular taxis in Hong Kong are metered. It’s hard to tell the exact cost for the trip.

5. Too much stuff to carry on a plane?

Whether you live in a dorm room or you get your own little place in Hong Kong, you always end up having way more belongings compared to when you first entered Hong Kong. When you have to evacuate your room for moving or the end of a contract, it is going to be difficult to carry everything you own on a plane.

Use Boxful. It is a Hong Kong local storage service that can store your excess belongings in mint colored, plastic boxes. They come door to door to drop off empty plastic boxes and picking up filled ones. A single box costs only 29 HKD per month.

They also take in larger belongings for safekeeping at a reasonable price. Every foreign student at my school uses it. Check it out!

6. IKEA is not the answer to everything.

In my first year in Hong Kong, my fellow foreign first year students enjoyed visiting IKEA for their necessities. For small appliances or furniture, it is understandable. For smaller stuff such as scented candles or plastic containers, visit somewhere else! IKEA sells cheap furniture, not cheap everything. As a matter of fact, selling cheap furniture while selling expensive smaller things is the store's tactic.

The better substitute store is JHC (Japan Home Centre), which is popular among locals. The designs of JHC products may not be as Scandinavian or enticing to the followers of IKEA. Be that as it may, the price of everything is

definitely much more affordable to
students and short-term expats.
JHC can be found nearly in every
neighborhood in Hong Kong.
IKEA, not so much. Plus, it is always
crowded and you will not be able to
shop without being pushed at least once.
So if you are in need of small
necessities in your room such as plastic
containers or soap dishes, visit JHC
before your day trip to IKEA.

7. Massive sales in Hong Kong

For all you fashion lovers, Hong Kong is an excellent place to shop. There are a variety of malls and outlets to shop from. But most importantly, there are killer sales.

There are three main sales seasons in Hong Kong when prices drop by as much as 50 percent: ***Summer, Singles Day, and Chinese New Year.***

Summer Sales: Hong Kong's most exciting sales season takes place in the summer months between June and August. During these months, there are sales all throughout the city with shops extending their shopping hours to 10 p.m. or even as late as midnight. You can find discounts of over 50 percent, particularly on end-of-season fashion items. Summer is when most fashion labels launch their autumn and winter collections. Hence, shops cut prices on their spring and summer collection to clear the shelves. At Causeway Bay's Fashion Walk, for instance, local designer shops start sales to take unpopular items off their hands at seriously reduced prices. Big-name department stores, like Shanghai Tang and Lane Crawford, also use this opportunity to lower their prices during the summer months. Some shopping malls offer dedicated vouchers and coupons that can be used in their various shops.

Singles Day Sales: In the latter half of the year, the biggest sale among Hong Kong’s shops is the Chinese version of Black Friday: Singles Day. Every year on November 11, Singles Day is

China's unofficial holiday for every single men and women. It's basically the opposite of Valentine's Day and every other holiday, Singles Day is for single people to go out to attend parties and speed dating events at bars. Unlike its profound meaning, Singles Day has become known as a mega-sales day. The holiday now ignites massive price cuts at most online outlets that spill out from beyond Hong Kong and Mainland China to the rest of the world.

Chinese New Year Sales: Unlike Western culture, Christmas holiday shopping isn't really a thing in Hong Kong. There may be some sales, but nothing compares to the discounts that can be found leading up to and during the Chinese New Year holidays. The Chinese New Year holiday occurs in late January or early February. This is the biggest shopping season of the year in Hong Kong!

During this time, all you will see sale signs, discount percentages, and two-for-one offers. Another fun shopping culture in Hong Kong is the discount coupons in the red lai see envelopes, which are traditionally given out by stores in times leading to and during the Lunar New Year.

Where to Find Sales

Even if you are in Hong Kong during these sale seasons, you have to know where to go. You'll find the biggest price drops at Hong Kong's malls and the city's more upscale boutiques and designer stores. It is rare, but there are a few brands and shops that will not participate in the sales, so don't feel deceived if the shop you visit refuses to lower prices.

For sales on designer luxury goods, plan to make shopping trips around the Central district of Hong Kong Island, SoHo and Admiralty. Start your luxurious bargain hunt at the mall of Landmark Hong Kong in Central Hong Kong, Pacific Place in Admiralty, and Lee Gardens in Causeway Bay.

For mid-range fashion goods, look in areas like Causeway Bay, Kowloon area, and Tsim Sha Tsui for reasonable prices. Malls to visit in those areas include Times Square and Sogo in Causeway Bay; Moko Plaza and Langham Place in Kowloon; and Harbour City Mall in Tsim Sha Tsui.

8. Telecommunications

There are four main telecomm providers in Hong Kong: csl., China Mobile Hong Kong, Three and SmarTone.

csl.

csl. is the largest provider in Hong Kong. It offers 2G, 3G and 4G/LTE services for GSM international phones. Prepaid SIM cards can be purchased from official stores and approved resellers and credit can also be picked up from the same retailers. Your passport doesn't have to be shown for the SIM card to be activated but we advise you to take it along just in case.

China Mobile Hong Kong

China Mobile is the largest provider in the world, mainly due to its coverage across China. They also offer a platform solely for the Hong Kong market, and offer 2G, 3G and 4G/LTE services for GSM international phones. Prepaid SIM cards can be purchased from official stores and approved resellers and credit can also be picked up from the same retailers.

Three

Three is the third largest provider in Hong Kong. It offers 2G, 3G and 4G/LTE services for GSM international phones. Prepaid SIM cards can be purchased from official stores and approved resellers, and credit can also be picked up from the same retailers.

Three also offers free Wi-Fi to customers using the HK subway network.

SmarTone

SmarTone is the smallest provider in Hong Kong but has been rated one of the best for its service. From experience, most short-term expat friends of mine used this provider. It offers 2G, 3G and 4G/LTE services for GSM international phones. Prepaid SIM cards can be purchased from official stores and approved resellers and credit can also be picked up from the same retailers.

Some More Tips:

- Locals call a SIM card a “SIM Kaa” or “SIM”.
- Sometimes communication in English can be difficult with the shop employees. I advise you to write down what you want rather than to keep explaining. Especially when it is a complaint.
- Ask the sellers to set up the SIMs for you since they will know how to do it.
- I advise you to purchase your SIM card from official stores rather than from street sellers.
- Get to the shops early to receive better assistance and to avoid the crowds.
- You cannot apply for suspension of service/payment if you have a year/2-year data usage contract.

9. Ordering in

It's late, it's hot, it's raining. You might be feeling lazy, you may want to watch Netflix with your meal. There can be many reasons why you want to order in. There are 5 or 6 good food delivery apps in Hong Kong. The three most popular ones are FoodPanda, Deliveroo, and UberEats.

FoodPanda is the largest of all delivery apps, and is the longest running in Hong Kong.

Deliveroo is a close runner-up, and it is rapidly expanding its serviceable areas including Sham Shui Po, Kwai Fong and Tsuen Wan. Some users say the user interface is a lot easier to use than other apps. There are specific filters on allergies, type of cuisine and price so that the users can find better food for themselves.

UberEats is quite new, I remember I first met the app working at a restaurant in SoHo back in 2017. Uber Eats is also developing fast, it already services the Hong Kong Island, Kowloon and New Territories.

Confused about which app to get?
My tip is – get all three and subscribe to their email notifications. It won't cost you. It actually will help you save money!

All three apps have all different restaurants. There may be some overlapping restaurants who can afford to have all three delivery outlets. But in the case of small cha chaan tengs (local coffee shops) and restaurants, they will usually use one or two. So if you cannot find a restaurant that suits your appetite in that moment, try switching to another app and scrolling.

The reason for email subscription is that all three apps have different discounts. UberEats usually treats new users well by providing many coupons, such as free delivery coupons.

Aside from using the app, I have two tips for the actual process of delivery.

Do not trust the remaining time on the app. Sometimes it can say the food will be at the door in 10 to 15 minutes, and it ends up taking 30 to 40 minutes.

Always be ready to receive a phone call when you are expecting a delivery. The deliverymen are very busy people.

They will not stay if you don't pick up or return their calls. Usually they will call about 3 to 5 times before they leave. Even if they leave without delivery, you will be charged. You can contact customer services on the app, but usually they don't help much in this situation. So always be a certain level of alert when you are waiting on food from the apps.

10. Why are the streets so wet in Hong Kong?

There are three answers - Street shops, pets and the air conditioners - all mixed with the humid Hong Kong weather.

First of all, the streets of Hong Kong, especially in the most commercial areas, are routinely washed away with cleaning water trucks with immense amount of water gushing out from its rubber pipes. In the extremely humid weather in Hong Kong, that water does not dry away for many hours.

Next up are those small damp areas usually at the edge of the concrete that is always wet. You may be able to guess what it is already without me stating it. Yes, it is the urine of pet dogs. These are mostly found around residential areas. I personally see the wet spots a lot when I take a walk through Bonham road near Central. Many residents or dog sitters walk up and down that road with a water bottle. The water from the plastic bottle is usually dispensed onto the concrete after the dog has relieved itself, for cleaning purposes presumably. These are the damp areas that you do not want to step in.

Last up is the most commonly visible, exterior air conditioning. With homes and offices crammed into such a small city, there is usually no space for air conditioning to be placed inside the room. Most houses hang them on the wall outside the building, usually supported with a metal structure. So most of the water droplets that you felt on top of your head when it isn't raining are from air conditioners that have been switched on for a fairly longer time. They are also accountable for the big damp spots in the streets, usually in commercial areas.

11. Is Chung King Mansions really that dangerous?

Like you, I re-watched the esteemed Hong Kong movie director Wong Kar Wai's cinematic classic, Chung King Express right before coming to Hong Kong. Many of us landed fresh on Hong Kong land with a fantasy about Chung King Mansions, which is portrayed as somewhat gruesome but oddly charming.

When asking any local friends, they would probably advise you to not go there alone.

So, is Chung King Mansions really that dangerous?

According the The Economist, Chung King Mansions is like the Mos Eisley

Cantina from Star Wars. Others have described Chung King Mansions as colorful.

Yes, there are occasional criminal activities of drug smuggling and whatnot. Visiting the place would include the experience of being offered drugs a couple of times. Reviews from visitors say they can spot some of the illegal or unsafe activity go on in the mansions, but nothing really happens to the tourists.

So all in all, it is unsafe. But if you want to shop exotic artifacts from Asia or Africa, want to enjoy their cuisine, or just simply desperate to look for a cheaper hostel to stay, you can give visiting Chung King Mansions a try.

12. Some tips for Yum Cha/Having Dim Sum

Yum Cha is the word locals use which means ‘Drink Tea’, which I translate it personally as “Let’s go have some Dimsum”.
But having Yum Cha can be tricky for first timers because it entails so many deeply rooted habits of Hong Kong or China.

(1) Rinsing the dishes and cups
First time I went to have dim sum, I was so ready to start my afternoon snack with a hot cup of tea that was provided as soon as we sat down. Turns out that the warm brownish tea water in the metal kettle was for rinsing the dishes, chopsticks and cups. You may be wondering if they don’t thoroughly wash the dishes and expects us to clean

it before we eat. That is not the case. The dishes and cups are clean, but rinsing it at the table with hot tea is a culture that has been long followed in Hong Kong.

(2) Ordering Menus

In the extra local dimsum shops, ordering can also be tricky for foreigners.

From my experience, there are two kinds of ordering in a Dim Sum shop. First is by paper. This is most common. You check the boxes or write down the numbers of plates you wish and hand it over to the waiter. Another way is in my nearby shop in Kennedy Town. You take the bamboo steamers with freshly steamed dimsum from a corner where waiters will just stack them up. When you have finished eating, the cashier will count the number of steamers at your table and charge you on that. Kind of like how they run the conveyer belt sushi place.

(3) Pour tea for others before pouring into your own cup.

Maybe our readers from similar East Asian cultures like Korea or Japan may be familiar with this one.

Pouring tea for others first is a sign of basic politeness and correct table etiquette in Chinese culture, and is especially important if you are dining with elders or people you are not yet familiar with. In a similar vein, if you see that a steamer has only one piece of dim sum left, don't just grab it. It may seem redundant to leave the piece hanging, but it is considered gracious to urge others to have the last piece.

13. Ocean Park vs. Hong Kong Disneyland

These are the two beloved theme parks of Hong Kong. But the entrance fee is quite expensive.

Ocean Park for adults is HKD438 and for Children is HKD219.
Hong Kong Disneyland is even more expensive, HKD619 for adults and HKD458 for children.

There may be those of you who can afford the time and money to go to only one of these parks.

My personal advice: If you are going with a child or you're a big fan of Disney, visit Disneyland. Otherwise, go to Ocean Park.

While Disneyland may be a haven for children under the age of 10, it lacks the excitement that will entertain teens and adults. There are only two or three thrill rides, which visitors who are used to thrill rides of Six Flags or Universal Studios will surely not recognize them as thrilling. One of the highlights of Disneyland is the parade. It is as entertaining as parades in other Disneylands around the globe with a pinch of Hong Kong culture blended in.

On the other hand, Ocean Park is more suitable for our readers who are over the age of 10. It has many rollercoasters and action rides that provide the thrill and also an awesome view of the ocean since it being on top of a mountain in the southern part of Hong Kong Island.

The Ocean Park Cable Car is also an attraction loved by many. It will take you on a steep climb up the mountain showcasing another amazing ocean view. There are also animal parks and marine parks with shows for all ages.

14. Octopus Card Comes in Handy in Many Ways

The Octopus Card is pretty much the first thing you need in your wallet when you get to Hong Kong. You need it for the bus, you need it for the MTR, the tram, the ferry. So it's used on basically every transportation mode in Hong Kong except the taxi.

The Octopus card can also be used if you have at least a cent left in your card. It allows you to max out your Octopus card until it hits minus HK$50.

You can also use it at:

- Vending machines
- 7-Eleven (and its competitor, Circle K)
- Starbucks
- Fast food outlets (including McDonald's, KFC, and other chain restaurants)
- Bakeries
- Car parks
- Supermarkets

Especially in supermarkets, using an Octopus may help you stay out of the big lines as you can use self check-outs, for those of you who have yet to possess a credit card.

15. Explore.

The last tip I want to give out is that don't limit yourself to the most comfortable areas just because you are used to it. Clean and shiny new malls in Central or Causeway Bay may feel enough. It is not true.

Try stepping into a wet market.

Wet markets are where regular Hong Kong people shop everything they eat. Fresh fish, meat, fresh veggies to cooked noodles, sushi, fruit and dry goods. And they are super cheap. Discover the most authentic sweets of the city: Hong Kong Egg Waffles, Egg Custard Tarts, Chinese Steamed Buns, Pineapple Buns and Dragon Fruit.

Other than the wet market, make it your goal to do something you haven't done in Hong Kong every week; visit Stanley, visit the markets in Prince Edward.

Though it is a small city, it has a lot more to offer than it seems.

Printed in Great Britain
by Amazon

62921612R10026